LOVING WISDOM

*Reflections on Cultivating
Fearless Conversations*

The Wisdom Whisperers
Henrietta Stith Andrews
Leslie Hazle Bussey
Joan Wagnon Drescher
Joyce Coleman Edwards
Zeresh Gosha
Rosalyn Roberts Mack
Michèle Mateno Silatchom
Beatrice Hunter Pack
E. Paulette Smith-Epps
Gail Tusan Washington

LOVING WISDOM

Reflections on Cultivating Fearless Conversations

By The Wisdom Whisperers

Henrietta Stith Andrews, Leslie Hazle Bussey, Joan Wagnon Drescher, Joyce Coleman Edwards, Zeresh Gosha, Bensonetta Tipton Lane, Rosalyn Roberts Mack, Michèle Mateno Silatchom, Beatrice Hunter Pack, E. Paulette Smith-Epps, and Gail Tusan Washington

Published by Hundredfold Return Publishing LLC

www.hrp-books.com

ISBN: 978-1-959130-18-5 *(Hardcover)*
ISBN: 978-1-959130-11-6 *(eBook)*

Printed in the United States of America

Hear what reviewers have to say about the third collection of Loving Wisdom...

Loving Wisdom, Reflections on Cultivating Fearless Conversations is more than a self-help guide; it is a companion for those navigating uncertainty. It does not promise to eliminate stress, nor does it offer pat answers. Instead, it invites the reader into a warm and genuine exchange across space and time—reminding us that we are not alone in our struggles. Whether you are seeking practical tools for managing daily anxiety or yearning for the comfort of knowing your experiences are shared, this collection offers both solace and strategy. It is a book to be savored slowly, a letter at a time, returning to its pages whenever the world feels heavy. For those seeking guidance and compassion in turbulent times, letters can sometimes serve as a source of resilience. They provide a beacon of hope and humanity.

Eleanor Murkey, Retired Dean of the College of Lake County, and Life Coach

Loving Wisdom, Reflections on Cultivating Fearless Conversations writes, "What defines us is not the labels we wear or the prayers we say but the compassion we give, the justice we seek, and the integrity we demonstrate." It speaks from lived experience and a deep understanding of the power of truth and love. The authors continue the examples of Ida B. Wells, Fanny Lou Hamer, and Maya Angelou in "Raising liberty's torch, by whose light we can see and tread a higher path to freedom and a more perfect union."

Pam Wylie Powell, Author of the forthcoming memoir, "Me Raising Me"

Loving Wisdom, Reflections on Cultivating Fearless Conversations is based on insightfulness, rooted in a sort of atmospheric instability called the unpredictable storm, caused by a chaotic shift within life. Tales of injustice have fragmented history passed down through generations. Prepare to feel the emotions of a melting pot of people and communities that develop in support of a restored nation called America.

Patricia Brown, Life Coach and Author of "A Woman's Inspiration"

ACKNOWLEDGMENTS

Former First Lady Michelle Obama reminds us that "Becoming isn't about arriving somewhere or achieving a certain aim…It instead [is a] forward motion, a means of evolving, a way to reach continuously toward a better self. The journey doesn't end." The Wisdom Whisperers recognize that others have influenced each of our *becoming*, and we pause to acknowledge the blessings received through those human connections and to express our abundant appreciation for their presence in our lives.

Henrietta Stith Andrews

I want to thank the numerous people who, unknowingly, assisted me over the course of many months in the process of writing this letter. They allowed me space in our conversations to explore the spiritual symbolism of *the arch of time*, which is central to my letter.

Special thanks to Bensonetta Tipton Lane and Rev. Lorraine McNeal for their editing insights and suggestions.

Joan Wagnon Drescher

I want to thank my sister, Susan, who was the inspiration for this essay. She has been there for me through thick and thin, the ups and downs, and the most challenging times of my life. We share a mother who instilled in us the importance of acceptance, open-mindedness, and honesty. These values have served us well.

Joyce Coleman Edwards

I want to thank several people who make it so easy for me to continue writing. My granddaughters, Sajdah, Ameera, and Khalilah, who inspired this piece and keep me on my toes every day. My friends Dee Alphabet, Dorcas Parham, and my sister-in-law, Terry, who keep me laughing and hold me accountable for staying true to myself! And lastly, my forever husband, Johnny, who continues to be the wind beneath my wings and a constant source of strength and inspiration.

Zeresh Gosha

Thanks to my parents, for whom I was their caregiver, for instilling in me the values of church, family, and community, and for always helping others along the way. I attribute my relationship with God, my successes, and my spirit of humanitarianism to them. In addition, I would like to thank my cousin and Fellow Wisdom Whisperer, Rosalyn Mack. She was there for me, holding me up, when I could not do it myself. Rosalyn introduced me to Wisdom Whisperers, and with her unwavering support, I have been able to navigate life's challenges and complete my first work as an author.

Rosalyn Roberts Mack

I dedicate my essay to everyone who played a role in my career in Corporate America. Special recognition is extended to the participants who joined me in the leadership engagement workshops focused on harnessing the performance impact of multi-cultural, global teams to drive results.

I truly appreciate the many skilled facilitators who guided and challenged us to confront our own biases, and encouraged us to truly listen, understand, empathize, and value the perspectives of others. I carry these learned skills with me even today.

I'm grateful for the honesty and candor of the Caucasian male participants who bravely gave voice to thoughts that are often left unspoken. Through that raw, courageous, and sometimes alarming dialogue, genuine understanding and growth emerged, enabling us to move forward as a more diverse and high-functioning organization.

Alongside my wonderfully insightful and supportive husband, Trentton K. Mack, who has been with me throughout my journey, I honor my dear friend and former colleague, Dr. Brenda Thomas Algee, who initiated our continued learning and exploration by inviting a group of phenomenal Black women to embark on this journey together. Now retired, we proudly call ourselves the Traveling Divas, as we continue to explore diverse cultures and regions of the United States. I feel truly blessed that these shared experiences have bound us together in sisterhood—one that has transcended both distance and time.

Beatrice Hunter Pack

I thank visionary Gail for the gift of writing with the Wisdom Whisperers, a talented sisterhood born during the pandemic, who share learned life experiences from the soul and prove once again that light shines brighter in darkness. Gail, you are unstoppable for all the right reasons. Thank you for daring greatly. A special thanks to Benni, a critical thinker and wordsmith - you challenge me to dig deeper as I write. To my husband, children, mom, dad, and family, I love you - you are my true community. I attribute who I am today to God and my beautiful, courageous mother. As an experienced mother, I understand your sacrifices; that is why I call you the Greatest Mom of All Time! Thank you, Dear Mother, for giving me the greatest gift – LOVE.

Michèle Mateno Silatchom

I want to express my deepest gratitude to Gail Tusan Washington for inviting me to be part of this collection of essays.

A special thank you to past and present Wisdom Whisperers for their encouragement and support.

I am especially grateful to Lala Deyoko, the first to whisper into my ears that I should write. Rose Hamadi Soumaré for more than thirty years of friendship. Sophie Kamenan for her support and prayers, and Anne Collins Smith.

Finally, I dedicate my heartfelt appreciation to Phil Keller, Dawn Bournand, Yulin Lee, Diane Bita Minsili, my people at the Eglise de la Sainte Trinité in Paris 9, my family, and God, without whom this journey would not have been possible.

E. Paulette Smith-Epps

I am indebted to my parents. They instilled in me a strong sense of self-worth, encouraged creativity, inspired me to love and appreciate life, and motivated me to strive for excellence, rather than settle for mediocrity. Even though they are no longer with us, their lessons still remain in my heart and soul. I will always be grateful to them. Rosalyn Roberts Mack was my group leader of the Dogwoods. She has been diligent in keeping us on track and providing us with pointers to help refine our essays. Thank you, Gail Tusan Washington, for inviting me to participate and contribute to this publication. The experience has been cathartic and phenomenal. I thank my family for giving me space and time to write and create. Finally, I thank my late husband, William Given Epps, Sr., who afforded me a wonderful life and family. Without his life, my essay would not have been possible.

Gail Tusan Washington

November 6, 2024, marked the beginning of *these challenging times,* as I had forecast for my two grandchildren and future generations. I am very proud of the Wisdom Whisperers' response to my challenge: "Write a letter to someone you care about and express how you personally are feeling post-election." Each of us wrote from the heart, revealing how we deal with the unknown and embrace reality beyond our control. As I reflect on the world in which we live and the impact of the actions taken on the federal, state and local level over the past several months, I am grateful for my husband, Carl and family, First Congregational Church, UCC, sister-friends, village of creatives and good trouble makers: Brown Sistahs Book Club, Buckhead/Cascade City (GA) Chapter, The Links Incorporated, Always Wanted To "AWT" Dance Troupe and Real Atlanta Golf Divas, PAVE, GLISI, my JAMS ADR team and JAMS Foundation colleagues. Thank you all for being willing to listen, commensurate, support, plot, strategize, dream, practice health and wellness, and model humanity at its best.

The Wisdom Whisperers greatly appreciate the editorial, creative, and technical assistance provided by our creative partners: our brilliant and intuitive editor, Monique Jewell Anderson, and our amazing and visionary publisher, Endeah Canty, and her talented team at Hundred-Fold Return Publishing. Thanks also to Bensonetta Tipton Lane, one of our own, who provided invaluable, tough-love first-read editorial advice to each of us, her Sister Whisperers. We thank our ride 'n dies: Velda North, Shirley Douglass, First Congregational Church, UCC, and the Brunswick Chapter (GA), the Links Incorporated, for your support along this third journey. Each of us wrote from a space of peace and hope, surrounded by our own network, which provided us inspiration, constructive feedback, practical advice, encouragement, positive energy, and grace. Finally, the Wisdom Whisperers are forever grateful for our readers. You encouraged us to whisper more. We listened and now offer you our third collection of reflections on being courageous in challenging times.

> *"We need to remember that we are all in this together, and that we have a shared responsibility to make our world a better place."*
> **– Lisa Murkowski**

TABLE OF CONTENTS

Despair and disbelief have swamped many people's feelings in 2025, countered only by professions of faith. Seasoned elders and students of history insist that greater challenges have been surmounted in the past so that we can survive the current calamities. This book allows a collective of women to investigate exactly what kind of faith and what lessons from collective or personal history might strengthen us all for the bumpy and treacherous road we travel.

Some of us are blessed to have living elders available to counsel us, but others can only imagine or remember what an elder might say to us in difficult times. This book offers surrogate elders, surrogate siblings, and even surrogate selves to offer wisdom. Whether these messages draw from sacred texts, familiar nonfiction, or unique ideas, they evoke strategies for achieving balance in the midst of unsettling events.

Unlike conversations, these written messages can be reviewed, annotated, and interrogated. Indeed, several of the contributors follow their works with discussion questions. The texts anticipate interaction. They are dynamic. The strategies require the reader's involvement. Whether the reader operates independently or within a book club or class, they will expand their thoughts and possibilities for successfully navigating whatever the current situation imposes upon us all.

While this book clearly addresses a specific moment in time, a particular political climate, and a designated nation, many of the concepts in this book will prove to be timeless and universal. Readers inevitably will emerge with renewed hope and may find themselves reaching out to others, so that the whispers reverberate.

Donna Akiba Sullivan Harper, PhD

INTRODUCTION

> *"Fight for the things that you care about,*
> *but do it in a way that will lead others to*
> *join you."*
> — **Justice Ruth Bader Ginsburg**

Loving Wisdom, Reflections on Cultivating Fearless Conversations, is our third collection of writings, building on the gifts that our growing collective of twenty-three women, the "Wisdom Whisperers," generously share with our audience of readers. When we embarked on the journey that resulted in the publication of the first volume five years ago, none of us imagined that the sharing–whispering of our voices and experiences would resonate as profoundly as they have. Over the past half-decade, the world navigated the once-in-a-lifetime event of a global pandemic. Since then, our country and the world have faced unprecedentedly challenging times in politics, economics, and society. Humanity is being tested. Normalcy has been tossed aside. The vulnerability of the American rule of law has been revealed. God is speaking. But who is listening? Have we taken for granted too much for too long and now find ourselves sucker punched and afraid to speak up practically everywhere?

Regardless of one's politics or worldview, a transformational event took place on November 5, 2024. We all saw it coming. Had the world not watched a grassroots call to arms four years prior? Yet, beginning with the day after the 2024 Presidential Election, shock, disbelief, disappointment, and mourning joined forces in response to gleeful relief, excitement, retribution, and a high-level systemic battle plan for change.

On November 6, 2024, I tuned in to hear Madam Vice President Kamala Harris speak masterfully and thoughtfully to all willing to listen. And then I turned off the television and logged onto my computer to issue a challenge to my Sister Warrior Wisdom Whisperers: "I want you to write a letter to whomever you choose and speak from your heart about how you are feeling in this moment."

> *"The United States of America is the greatest idea humanity ever devised. A nation big enough to encompass all our dreams, strong enough to withstand any fracture or fissure between us, and fearless enough to imagine a future of possibilities."*
> — **Kamala Harris**

This book is the result of their prompt acceptance of my challenge. Everyone said yes! And there lies the beauty of our pages herein. We were deeply affected by the election. Everyone cares about their country, family, village, and beyond. Like you, your neighbors, co-workers, friends and loved ones, we do not think uniformly, we do not always express our thoughts clearly, we might inadvertently offend or intentionally respond in anger but deep down, as the late U.S. Representative Barbara Jordan reminds us, "What the [We, the] people want is simple: they want an America as good as its promise."

Recently, on a wonderful visit home to Altadena, one of those truly great communities in our country, I heard a sermon by a guest minister at my childhood church, Scott United Methodist Church. He spoke about the emancipation from the habit of hesitation and the crippling effect that fear and apathy can have on one's life. Quite coincidentally, his name was Rev. Washington. His beautifully crafted sermon was uplifting and, for me, timely as I contemplated writing this introduction. He preached using the analogy of a whisper in one's ear by someone you love and trust, and how their own fear, bias, and insecurities are passed on to you in that whisper. Your behavior is often conditioned by what you hear, especially if you are young or living a sheltered existence at the time. Over time, the whispered advice can become second nature and may even become limiting. As I paraphrase what I heard, the practical life skill and takeaway is this: we must all assume the role of ambassadors for humanity. We must commit to being active listeners, curious learners, and intentionally remain open to a change of view, even about those people, experiences, and facts we might consider ourselves to be *right*. Just as the minister cautioned that we can unknowingly allow a whisper to cripple or paralyze us, the Wisdom Whisperers present this book as a counterbalancing collection of whispers that call out the innate human tendency to hope, inspire, empathize, and act for the common good. We want our readers to overcome the fear, doubt, or ambivalence that we all experience from time to time.

What started as a collection of letters facilitating personal venting, screaming, sobbing, cursing, and praying within the nurturing and creative haven of the Wisdom Whisperers has evolved into this book. We felt it was vital for you to read our actual letters, but pushed ourselves to give our audience much more. As you turn the pages, you will find inspiring quotes, our reflections, conversation starters, helpful tips on engaging in productive discussions, and other gems of wisdom lovingly passed on from the collective to you and your networks, families, and friends. We invite you to join us in facilitating fearless conversations in these challenging times.

Be prepared to be flooded with a range of emotions as you read our letters and assume the place held by the recipient of each missive. Perhaps sentiments are residing in your subconscious, awaiting action on your part to be put into words on paper or articulated through the stroke of a keyboard. Not surprisingly, there may be someone you have wanted to call or send a note to over the past several months as you have scrolled through your social media feed or watched a news program in response to the reality drama unfolding across our country. Loving Wisdom, a

Second Collection, concluded with a letter from God addressed to anyone, if not all of us. Whisperer Roberta Jackson envisioned what the Creator might say. In this collection, ten Wisdom Whisperers have written letters and poems filled with love, concern, counsel, and wisdom based on their own experiences of coping, adapting, hoping, persevering, and living alongside an unfamiliar narrative of what is excellent. The authors continue their Loving Wisdom storytelling tradition with this new thought-provoking twist.

The reader first encounters a letter of encouragement from the higher self to Rosalyn Roberts Mack, in which she reflects on her thoughtful and measured response to the outcome of the 2024 Presidential Election. Faced with concerns about the nation's direction, Roz is commended for her conscious efforts to find peace by limiting news and political discussions, refusing to speculate, and seeking spiritual guidance. The wisdom gleaned from her letter explores: Responding to unexpected events with reflection and intentional action, protecting your peace, drawing on trusted sources of wisdom, and reflecting deeply on these sources to find clarity and strength as you navigate challenging times.

A particularly poignant letter penned by a French

African immigrant to her younger self reflects on the election and the feeling of powerlessness. Identity and gender are at the center of her writing as she chronicles three decades of personal growth. Now, facing a crossroads in her life pursuits, she muses on why her dreams are being deferred and for how much longer.

In an effort to comprehend the unfathomable, Joan Drescher writes to her sister, Susan, as she tries to process, understand, and believe what for her was an American nightmare. In her letter, she suggested a few ways to move forward and reclaim control of our own lives. She emphasizes the importance of surrounding ourselves with a strong support system made up of people we trust and can turn to for help. Her letter calls for a resurgence of volunteerism and community activism.

The actual process of writing these letters was a challenging and emotional exercise. Not far into this project, we all discovered that our letters were not easy to pen because the historic event and impetus for this book triggered strong guttural reactions. Unlike the January 6, 2021, insurrection on the steps of the United States Capitol, Loving Wisdom: Reflections on Cultivating Fearless Conversations is not an impulsive tantrum made in response to a political event. As Joyce Coleman Edwards writes to her granddaughters, our goal is to convey pearls of wisdom. In her letter, she emphasizes the importance of practicing self-care, work-life balance, and leaning into friendships during times such as these. Just as women in her circle cared enough to keep her informed and help her avoid various pitfalls, Edwards pays it forward to the next generation.

Writing to my two grandchildren (ages 8 and 5), who were very much aware of the campaign season culminating with the 2024 Presidential Election, I do my best to redirect their attention from the startling result of the election to the role they can play in reframing the future and leading us as representatives of Generation Alpha.

Calling out to all of God's children, E. Paulette Smith-Epps offers coping strategies to help navigate the uncertain times we will undoubtedly face, guiding the reader through unexpected, chaotic, and uneasy times. She hopes that her letter will be a blessing, providing peace of mind and fostering a healthy appreciation for life, family, and God's creation.

Reverend Henrietta Stith Andrews' letter reflects

on the emotional and societal impact of the 2024 presidential election. She felt personally diminished by the results and was subsequently challenged to respond to her own feelings. Standing up for what one feels is right is not always easy. Andrews suggests being aware of one's gifts, i.e., what is unique about each one of us, as a starting point. In this letter, she imagines herself as part of a long line of folk who, for centuries, have worked to name themselves and persevered together toward a common goal, not always realized in their lifetime.

Zeresh Gosha's letter provides a rare glimpse at the personal experiences of a Veteran and Army Nurse, and how politics affects the boots on the ground in terms of the well-being of service members during their active service and beyond.

Beatrice Hunter Pack reflects on the America she remembers and the changes underway, and how the swift disposal of established processes and excessive reliance on executive orders cause uncertainty in our nation and unfamiliarity even among people she knows and loves. Pack's letter is addressed to the community, family, and friends, and in her search for truth, peace, and understanding, she issues a passionate call for survival. Faced with choices, this

Whisperer elected to raise her pen and voice to engage in difficult conversations, founded on our similarities rather than differences.

> *"These are challenging times at home and around the world. We will have to work together in a bipartisan spirit and with our international partners if we are going to achieve progress and peace now and for future generations."*
> — **Susan Collins**

Through Pack's letter and the others, we remind our readers of America's promise: "We, the people, for the people." Join the Wisdom Whisperers as our voices are heard through active listening, voting, organizing, petitioning, and advocacy. No one person, elected or self-anointed, nor their political party, nor a piece of legislation, nor an executive order, is going to redirect our path forward singularly. Each of us must commit to helping shape the future and pave the way for our grandchildren and future generations. Together, we can contribute to a healthier society; together, we win.

Finally, we would be thrilled for you to read this book with your book club and invite you to sit down and have a conversation prompted by one or more of the enclosed letters with family, friends, coworkers, neighbors, or a stranger you might encounter while traveling. A Guide for Conversation has been included at the back of this book for your consideration. A listing of discussion questions follows each letter.

Like love, wisdom is best when it is shared, and humanity, civility, and the rule of law are preserved through courageous, fearless, two-way conversation. Maya Angelou wrote, "You may not control all the events that happen to you, but you can decide not to be reduced by them."

1

My Letter to Myself

by

Rosalyn Roberts Mack

> *"I am not a product of my circumstances.*
> *I am a product of my decisions."*
> — **Stephen R. Covey**

> *"We may encounter many defeats, but*
> *we must not be defeated."*
> — **Maya Angelou**

Congratulations, Roz!

I am so proud of you. Although the outcome of the November 5th, 2024, Presidential Election took you by surprise, you responded with careful reflection and intentional action, considering both the significance and the possible consequences of the results.

You continue to carry many concerns—among them, the nation's gradual slide toward autocracy, the growing prioritization of wealth and power over strong moral and ethical principles, and the troubling signal sent to future generations that character and integrity may no longer matter.

I commend you for the steps you chose to take:

- Reducing your exposure to commentary and pundit-driven news programs

- Limiting political discussions with friends and family

- Refusing to speculate about the future

- Seeking spiritual guidance and wisdom

These choices will help restore your sense of peace and stillness. I encourage you to revisit the sources of wisdom that have guided you through past challenges—three books in particular come to mind. First, Lillian Smith's Killers of the Dream offers profound insights into the enduring impact of rigid cultural frameworks, the lessons learned in Southern society, and the complexities of Southern racism.

Lessons from Killers of the Dream

I recall that you were first introduced to Lillian Smith's book, "Killers of the Dream," while working for DuPont. You and some of your colleagues were seeking to appreciate cultural differences better. Although published in 1949, it provides an insightful analysis and critique of the pre-1960s American

South; its analogies informed your comprehension of the policies proposed by the nation's current leaders. Smith, herself a white Southerner, expressed a fear that we may remain bound by past mistakes, wondering whether destroying the dream of a just world might ultimately lead to our downfall. She posed questions that continue to resonate today: Can we endure a dead dream within us? How many dead dreams will it take to destroy us all?

Smith chronicles lessons learned from birth in the South, deeply embedded with the expectation of conformity: being both gentle and callous, praying at night, then riding Jim Crow cars by day, celebrating democracy while practicing slavery—all while feeling comfortable doing both. This duality was taught, and conformity was expected, until the mind, heart, and conscience became shut off from one another and from reality. Unless confronted, this history fosters persistent behaviors rooted in racism, sexism, and other "isms" that have the potential to fester and undermine our *civilized* society.

Second was Stephen Covey's "The Seven Habits of Highly Effective People." It explores perspective and how it shapes our views of one another.

Stephen Covey on Paradigms: **Do You See What I See?**

Although the ability to dance with dual and competing realities was passed down through generations, resulting in many 'isms', there are often other factors to consider. Did Donald Trump supporters see his actions the same way you did? What did his supporters hear when he demeaned certain people? Was Project 2025 read? If so, what did they perceive? As they say, one's perception is their reality. Roz, do you recall the explanation of the concept of Paradigm Shift described in Stephen Covey's Seven Habits? It helps explain why some of your friends, people you respect and trust, can observe behavior you deem disrespectful, yet perceive it differently. Both of you may be right. Covey explains that the way we perceive things is the source of how we think and act. Roz, what about the illustration on paradigms in Covey's book of a woman who can be seen as both old and young, depending on how you look at her? What did you see? An old woman? Correct! A young woman? Correct! Yes, both are right – it's not logical, it's psychological. There's a need for everyone to recognize their own paradigms—the way we see, understand, and interpret the world—because it's the source of how we think and act. Covey also suggests that an attempt to '...change outward attitudes and behaviors does very little good in the long run if we fail to examine the basic paradigms from which those attitudes and behaviors flow.' To successfully navigate the challenges faced in the United States, the country needs not only to focus on attitudes and behavior but also to do the difficult work of critical discernment and excavating (when required) the root paradigms from which our attitudes and behaviors flow. Roz, this is challenging work – like the work you've done over many decades. Please note that many people refuse to explore their paradigms, let alone shift them.

Ultimately, the Bible, your steadfast source of faith, offers insight into what God would have us do in times like these.

There is Good News

The journey that you, individually and collectively as a society, are being called to take has existed for centuries. Rev. Dr. Howard-John Wesley's sermon, "I've Got Some Good News", summarized it well. He reminds us that Luke 2:8-20 describes the Good News about Jesus' birth. It was during the reign of Caesar Augustus that God decided it was time to birth a new

King. He sent angels to shepherds living in fields outside the city of Bethlehem to deliver the Good News of the coming of Christ. Like the shepherds, God often uses people whom others have rejected. Did you notice that God didn't involve Kings or other dignitaries, but instead sent angels to the shepherds? God has a way of finding and working through people in the fields. Additionally, Rev. Wesley reminds us that there are at least 500 messianic prophecies in the Old Testament, which are promises and predictions of the coming of Christ. However, during the Intertestamental Period, the 400 years between the recorded writings of the Old and New Testaments, it was said that God was silent. There were no promises, no prophecies, and no prophets. Nothing. Could the United States and the world be in a similar era now? The behavior is similar: doubt, wonder, lost hope, and fading faith. But remember, Roz, God always performs what God promises. Just as the angels came to the shepherds and said, 'TODAY, God did what He promised He would do.' It doesn't matter how long it takes - if God said it, He will do it. God is able. Have faith that God is always working things out for good. Give God time - let Him fix things in His timing. I challenge you to march into the future determined to see God do what God can do. As it states in 2 Chronicles 7:14, "If my people who are called by my name humble themselves and pray and seek my face and turn from their wicked ways, then I will hear from heaven and will forgive their sin and heal their land."

Though the work before you may appear daunting, stay strong, be well, and seek God to order your steps. God will heal your land, and you will overcome.

Roz, continue to reflect deeply on each of these sources as you navigate these times and seek more profound wisdom and clarity.

With blessings, faith, and peace,

Your Higher Self

Rosalyn Roberts Mack

Discussion Questions

1. What lessons from your past have helped you through tough times—and do you think they would help now?

2. Can you recall a time when a particular story, book, or piece of wisdom helped you find meaning or solace in a difficult moment? How did it make a difference?

3. What boundaries or limits do you set—whether with people, media, or your own thoughts—to protect your peace in the midst of chaos?

4. In what ways has your perspective on leadership, honesty, or courage evolved as you've navigated recent challenges, and how do you communicate those insights to others?

5. What routines or boundaries do you rely on to keep your head clear and stay grounded when the world feels chaotic?

6. How have changes in what society values shaped the way you talk about honesty and good leadership with others?

2

A Letter to Mi

by

Michèle Mateno Silatchom

NONE

Dear Mi,

This is Mich, also known as 2MS or MMS, writing to you from the future, 30 years from now, to be exact.

Blissful ignorance is how I would qualify your mindset as you woke up this morning, November 2024. You are hopeful, but there is a lingering gut feeling in your stomach. You don't know why, but the lyrics of the song "Losing My Religion, by the rock band R.E.M., are coming to mind. "Oh, life is bigger, bigger than you, and you are not me…" You brush it off until suddenly you see a headline on YouTube, and you read, "…delivered the victory to …"

Your dreams, your present, your future … Your life. People have decided to return to madness and make decisions that are detrimental to basic decency.

Michèle, as you read this letter, we have gone back to 1994, when you were a chubby junior in high school in the 4ème arrondissement in Paris, the proud eldest daughter of immigrants from the Bamiléké tribe in Cameroon (Central Africa). You were feasting on *The Soul of MTV* and *Yo MTV Raps*, singing, "The best things in life are free," and dancing to *Papa Bonheur*, while avidly watching the world events unfolding.

You became an activist in middle school after reading the works of Patrick Chamoiseaux, Toni Morrison, Malcolm X, and Mayse Condé, and witnessing the ravages of the AIDS Epidemic and economic crises.

Not only were you enmeshed in French politics, but you were also simultaneously absorbed by global events. You were exhilarated to no longer be the token person of color in class; you had met and participated in education alongside classmates from diverse backgrounds and ethnicities. This is the end of a century, and you were filled with optimism when you read that a young, free-spirited saxophonist had been elected President of the United States of America. Nelson Mandela was now the head of State in South Africa. Those events gave you hope for the future of the French presidential elections after two seven-year terms from a president who was aging.

However, you will quickly become disillusioned when a year later, in May of 1995, the French people chose to veer right - more conservative, more bourgeois. Like a lot of young people, you will feel betrayed and powerless since you are not yet eligible to vote. You will find yourself sitting on the dock of the bay.

All is not lost, Mi, because one day, you're going to

live in A-me-ri-ca! After studying law, you will become the new Jimmy Sifuentes. Indeed, normally, by the next French presidential elections, you will be legally considered an adult, have completed your education, and be eligible to vote so you can make your voice heard.

Unfortunately, Ma Chère Mi, things will not be any better. After surviving a strange election cycle in the US (where are those ballots, Florida? Like Joe, "I wanna know") and the Y2K bug, the world will witness live, two planes strike the Twin Towers in New York, one drop on the Pentagon, and a new war in Afghanistan in the Fall of 2001.

After casting your vote in various local elections, 2002 will mark the first time that you are voting for presidential elections, and by the end of that year, you will pass the Bar.

On this fateful Sunday of April, you spend your afternoon feeling confident that it will be a new day, a new Dawn. Still, at 8 PM, you will watch on TV as they announce the result of the first round, that the Neo Nazi party is on the doorstep of the Elysée. Dumbstruck, you put your hand on your head while reading in the sidebar at the bottom of the TV screen.

More than 25% of the population did not even take the time to go to the polls. Instead, they preferred to enjoy the green space on this sunny Sunday of Spring, persuaded that the government from the left had given the people many advantages and benefits, and would likely pass and go to the second round.

Again, a majority, by their nonchalance, will have a negative impact on your life.

Most of the people who voted did not do so out of hatred, but rather to be contrarian, forgetting that the desire and yearning to stand out can have a negative impact on others.

These circumstances will echo in the US in 2016.

Ironically, after three presidential elections in France and a slew of elections in the US with various incredible outcomes (including the election of the First Black President), you will finally obtain a visa and land in Boston, Massachusetts, in the Summer of 2017 to finally live your American dream.

Even though you reside in a pocket of liberalism, you will witness the fear and the uncertainty of a life when power has been given to a bunch of lunatics after the election of #45. You will feel uneasy about being othered in a society that held promise for you to become whoever you wanted. You will face an existence where conformity is not enough, and denial is required to mitigate the uneasiness of being another.

A small glimmer of hope happens with the midterms in 2018, and for two years, you will cling to that window. Then a hitherto unseen global pandemic arrives and puts the world on its knees. An act as natural as breathing would become a death sentence.

We are in 2020, and you have been in your dream for more than three years. You are now faced with uncertainty, disillusionment, and a lack of understanding of what you have experienced. By September, you may feel unworthy, wanting to give up and return to where you came from. You feel like you cannot *Stomp* and do not have the strength to "clap your hand and want to dance." Your American Dream has evolved into a better video clip than the one used for the song 'The Disappointed' by XTC.

Come November, after a lockdown and a summer of recollection, you can hear everywhere "F.D.T." (expletive, Donald Trump) and strike up the YouTube video, "You bout to lose your job."

You feel that better days are coming, or at least

you think so. You feel relieved, despite COVID-19 still being prevalent and deadly. In the following months and years, you will witness a world tending more and more to the far-right and curling up. Sordid ideas and disinformation will take the lead, and in the year 2024, you will witness the unfathomable. Idiocracy and a convicted felon becoming the leader of the *free world*...again! You will cry, and hopelessness will creep in again, hindering all aspects of your life.

That is the mindset in which I am putting these words.

Mich (yes, I add a "C" and a "H" to your nickname because I Care and want to see you Happy). I realized that I may have scared you with this letter.

However, my intent is less about giving a historical retrospective of the last three decades between your homeland and your dreamland, but to warn you of how often you will leave yourself impacted by the outside circumstances and delegate your destiny.

"Ma Chère Mich," despite all the above, the disasters and tragedies that you will experience in the next 30 years, you are still standing. As Mobb Deep sang, "Only the strong survive." And you, Mich, you are strong, resilient, and deserving. As you contemplate the following steps, the results of the 2024 elections will make you realize that this American Dream has become a journey of digging from within and exhaling a new YOU.

Despite the noises and the collective madness that can and may happen around you, you do not have to let the stuttering of History impact your life and your decisions. As Nasir Jones said, "The world is yours."

Go and create your furrow in the tempest that is called life.

Michèle Mateno Silatchom

Conversation Starters and Reflective Questions

1. Are the elections the only moment to be involved in the community?

2. How does it feel to be "othered" by your community? How does one outgrow the reflection of the majority?

3. What does "Not survive but thrive" (in the words of Maya Angelou) look like for you?

4. How does one avoid oscillation between high hopes and desperation?

5. What are some practical ways to support individuals (teens not eligible to vote, felons, immigrants, etc.) whose voices are not recognized through the democratic process?

6. For members of a majority: What does "allyship" look like?

3

A Letter to My Sister, Susan

by

Joan Drescher

> *"In the cookies of life, sisters are the chocolate chips."*
> — **Unknown**

Dear Susan,

Hello! I hope this letter finds you, Bill, the kids, and the grands all doing well. I know that we have been struggling since Trump was elected just a few days ago. I am writing to share some of my thoughts. We were excited and hopeful after Kamala Harris entered the race. I know how we struggled with the four years that Trump was in power and couldn't begin to fathom another four years with him at the helm.

The fact that this country could elect someone who is a convicted felon, a bigot, and a narcissist who doesn't have the ability to feel empathy is appalling. This is an individual who has no respect for our Constitution. This became blatantly clear on January 6, 2021, when he encouraged and supported his followers to attack our US Capitol building in an attempt to stop Congress from certifying the electoral votes of the 2020 presidential election. This day of certifying the electoral votes and electing a new President had always been a peaceful transition. Lives were lost as a result of this mob attack. His attempt to call the election a fraud and his refusal to accept the results further showed who he truly is. An individual who denies the truth and is not fit to hold the position of the presidency and represent our country. I also found it mind-boggling, and still do, that so many people supported his accusations.

You and I were brought up by parents who showed us, by example, what it means to be a person of integrity, honesty, and empathy. We were taught to respect what our Founding Fathers stood for, fought for, and the ultimate democracy they created for this country.

Now that some of the initial shock has worn off and the reality has settled in that we are stuck with this convicted felon for the next four years, I'm left with "How do we cope and navigate these next four years?" I have decided to focus on a few key areas that I believe will help me going forward, and I am sharing them with you in the hope that you will find them helpful. I welcome your response and thoughts.

Firstly, it is essential to prioritize and take control. We need to focus on our own lives and what is essential. Also, we need to claim and take control of our own thoughts, feelings, and actions. Ultimately, it is up to us as to how we handle this challenging time. Indeed, for me, what is most important is my family. I know how important your family is to you. We have been blessed with wonderful husbands, great kids, and fabulous grandchildren. Trump is a man who is far from a role model for our children and grandchildren. We must carefully help our children and grandchildren understand this. I'm not going to let my frustrations and anger over Trump cloud and control who I am at my core and what is truly important. I see the need to acknowledge these negative feelings and learn how to transform them into positive ones.

Another goal is to surround ourselves with people we trust, who will be there for us during the ups and downs and will always have our backs. We need the love and support that comes from a strong, supportive group. Finding someone in our friend and family group with whom we can share our feelings might be helpful. Someone who can help us sort out the negative and not let this crazy man make us crazy!

In addition, we need to keep our priorities in perspective and stay the course. It's easy to get sucked into the chaos. I don't believe that will benefit us in any way. There are so many unsettling and sad things happening in this complex world right now. It's important to have an overall awareness, feel empathy, and give support when we can, but we cannot allow ourselves to become overwhelmed by it all.

Lastly, I will use this time as an opportunity to challenge myself. I am choosing not to focus on the negative, but to become purposeful with my actions. I am resuming my volunteer work at the monthly VA food distributions. It is amazing and rewarding to meet so many giving people and to help others. I have also started volunteering with a wonderful non-profit, CURE Childhood Cancer. By volunteering and giving of my time, my goal is to connect with my community. I want to show my grandchildren what is truly important in life, which is not reflected in Trump's words or actions. I want to lead by example.

I know that for you, God, your faith, and your church are of great importance. I hope these are all providing you solace. It's essential to have a strong support system, and I'm glad you do.

I have recently thought about Mom. She would be equally upset over this current US political situation. She always set a wonderful example by her willingness to take on a challenge and find solutions. We watched as she fought for equal rights and showed us the importance of treating everyone with respect and dignity. I remember as a young child going with Mom when she picked up children to take them to a Head Start program. The values she displayed were deep, and I'm proud to say, have helped me be a better person. I wish she were here to give us encouraging words to help us deal with all of this.

I keep telling myself that, fortunately, this will not last forever. These next four years will occur. Many things are beyond my control, and I need to accept this. I may not agree with many or most of what happens, but it is up to me as to how I react. I can become proactive by contacting my government representatives and bringing my concerns to their attention. They are elected officials who are supposed to listen to and act on behalf of their constituents. This is how our Democracy works. We must continue to believe in the system and fight for its existence.

Getting these thoughts down in writing helps me sort out how I will present myself and navigate the next four years. I hope you can find some benefit and encouragement in my words, as you have always been there for me. My focus will be on what is important, turning to others for support, giving back, and maintaining a positive outlook.

I am so fortunate to have you as my sister. I know that we will be there for each other, and for that I am grateful.

I love you.

Joan

Joan Drescher

Questions

1. What was your initial reaction when you found out that Trump had been elected as President?

2. Who would you write a letter to?

3. What advice would you give that person?

4. Are you using the same advice you give to others?

5. How can we come together and support each other?

4

A Letter to My Granddaughters, Saldah, Ameera, and Khalilah

by

Joyce Coleman Edwards

> *"Always aim high, work hard, and care deeply about what you believe in. When you stumble, keep faith. When you're knocked down, get right back up. And never listen to anyone who says you can't or shouldn't go on."*
> — **Hillary Clinton**

Dear Ladies,

2024 was a rough year for me and the world around me. I have spent a lot of time coping with the underlying stress of what was happening—personal loss of friends and family, as well as all kinds of upheaval all over the world. For a few months, I was hopeful but cautious that a Black woman would be elected president, and the world would avoid a man with no moral compass or compassion for anything other than money and power. Unfortunately, our hopes were dashed, and now we are stuck for four more years with 'Problem Child, 2.0. I must admit that I was not shocked about the outcome, just disappointed that some have no problem with a man who calls people terrible names, cheats on his wives, and has not an ounce of compassion for anyone who is not wealthy or affluent. Out of the gate, he is doing his absolute best to make the United States and the world an extremely dangerous place. At the same time, I am still trying to cope with the fallout, disappointment, and sadness of knowing that half the people in the United States are okay with a leader who is dishonest, money hungry, and has no real intention of making this country a better place for all its residents. It is hard to fathom how things have gotten so crazy. Unfortunately, we have allowed outside forces and the media to determine how we think, live, and react to any given situation. We have been so desensitized to the violence and terrible things going on in our society that we do not even blink anymore when we hear about these things happening. We accept that this is how it is, and we must deal with it. Money and influence have taken the place of morals and doing what is right. Guns and violence have become so commonplace that we have talked ourselves into thinking that if we do not have a weapon, we are not safe, even though there are a lot of countries that believe in gun control and have little gun violence. Second Amendment rights have replaced common sense!

So, why am I writing this letter to you? My concerns for you and your future are felt deeply real by me. I am in the fall of my life, whereas you are just beginning yours. There are things I want to ensure you are aware of while I have the opportunity to inform you. So, to start, I am asking you the question, "Why should you care about the rest of your life now?"

At ages 18, 22, and 24, you are at the very beginning of figuring out what you want to do, who you want to be, and how you are going to get there. At 17, I was graduating from high school, preparing to attend college, and considering a career as a lawyer. At 20, I joined the Air Force Reserves after leaving college. By the time I turned twenty-three, I was planning a wedding and working for the phone company, where I thought I would retire in thirty years. At 26, I was a mom and made the move from Chicago to Atlanta.

If I could go back and change things, I would have taken a year off from college. I would have graduated and figured out a career in the Air Force. I wish I had known how hard it was to keep a marriage together or be a working mom. I got married for the sake of getting married. Not giving myself time to know more about life, and not settling for just any relationship, but a real one with a person who would champion and encourage me to be my best self. I struggled in my marriage until I made up my mind that there was something or someone better. I left with my child, divorced, and set off to continue my life as a single mom. Not knowing that a few years later, my life would take a drastic turn, leaving me alone with no ex-husband and no child.

Life has a way of waking you up and turning your life around in seconds. It happens so fast you barely have time to take it all in before the next thing comes up. You are in the spring of your lives, and you have all the time in the world to do all the things that you dream of doing. You will find that life has taken you to some places you did not want to go, but in the struggle of it all, you found a way to make all your dreams come true. That is why you should care about the rest of your life now.

Recent events have raised concerns about your well-being. Black women are the most educated group in our country at present. But we are also the most undervalued, underpaid, and most sexualized. Events like reversing Roe vs Wade and limiting adequate contraceptives can easily derail a dream and cause unnecessary pain and suffering. Not having control of our own bodies is something I never thought would be reversed in my lifetime, but here we are. Because of this, research for women, especially women of color, is way behind the research for the other genders and most of society. We contract more illnesses, diseases, and other medical issues than any other race or gender. Often, we are denied healthcare, or when we complain of symptoms, we are usually placated or ignored. Black women die disproportionately more during childbirth than other races and receive the worst care. With that said, be sure to take care of yourself, both medically and emotionally. Do not be afraid to ask questions if you feel something is not right. If the medical provider is vague or gives answers that don't sit right with you, consider consulting with another provider. You cannot have a productive life if you do not self-advocate and self-care. You cannot be your best self if you are not healthy.

I am not sharing these issues with you to scare you, but to make you aware, so you will know for which to fight. Racism in the country is raging along with sexism. A lot of what I am telling you now has not changed since I was your age, or my mother's, or my grandmother's. With every generation, there is hope that things will get better. Do not get me wrong, we have made great strides and advances since my grandmother and mother were your age. However, our civil rights are being rapidly eroded or altered, so that we no longer have the same liberties that others enjoy in our society. We are often the last to be hired and the first to be fired, despite having the most education and experience. In the workplace, we are given the most to do with little or no assistance. We are pigeonholed into positions with little to no opportunities for advancement. When we ask to be considered for better assignments and promotions, we are told we are not qualified, even though we have been doing the job in the interim while they search for someone else. Then, when they hire someone else, they ask us to train them.

I want better for you. I want you to be cognizant of your surroundings, know your worth, and not accept the first or second suggestion from just anyone. Know the difference between wisdom and a selfish suggestion. Reach for what you want and don't let anyone steer you away from it. Share your ideas with only those who encourage you without judgment and offer help to reach your goal. Learn to say less and listen more. When someone gives you a piece of wisdom, please don't throw it away, tuck it away! Eventually, you will need it later in life. Your generation is smarter than mine in so many ways. You will not sit on a job that is not fulfilling, or take abuse from a weird manager, or get paid way less than your colleagues. You are not concerned with longevity on the job, but rather with achieving a good work-life balance and working in an environment that is beneficial for your health and well-being. I also want you to be economically healthy. Know how to manage money and how to make money. What I mean by that is to build informed financial decisions for both the present and the future. The time to think about retirement is now, not when you get into your 40s or 50s. By then, you are late in the game and will not have the time needed to save and invest so that you can live the same lifestyle when you are no longer working. Do not be afraid to invest in the stock market or have multiple income streams. The days of depending on others for our lifestyle are over. Circumstances can change at a moment's notice; women need to be prepared just like men for those life changes. Being financially stable will give you the confidence and courage to be your best self and pursue the things in life you truly want to achieve.

I also want you to be concerned about other Black women. We need to stop being so rigid and judgmental towards each other. We must learn to love each other for our strengths and weaknesses. We must share the good and evil and hold each other accountable with love. We have been beating ourselves and our sisters up too much, and we need to stop it! And it begins with you. Do not let your friend do something crazy without telling her there is a better way. Do not be the one to say, "I told you so," but be the one to hold her when she makes a mistake and help her make it right. Be her support even when she will not take your advice. Eventually, she will love you for it. And if she does not, that is not on you; you did your best.

I want you to know that one of the best gifts God has given me is granddaughters! I am so proud of you and all your accomplishments. You are strong, intelligent women who have bright futures. Hold on to your dreams, do not abandon them. Hold them tight and do not let anyone steer you away from what you want. Life is too short for "what ifs!" You cannot go back and change things, but you can go forward, using the past to shape the future. In response to the question, I posed at the beginning of this letter, I encourage you to start now and carve out the best life for yourself. Don't let it just happen - be intentional!

With much love and admiration,

Nana

Joyce Coleman Edwards

Discussion Questions

1. After reading Joyce's submission, which of her pearls of wisdom did you find to be most useful to share?

2. With all that's going on in the world, what are your gut reactions?

3. Feeling those reactions, do you feel compelled to do something, take some action?

4. What is your strength, and what's preventing you from sharing it with others?

5. This is more of a charge than a question. "Go change the World, you have what it takes to do so!"

5

A Letter to My Grandchildren, Kendall and Cameron

by

Gail Tusan Washington

Dear Kendall and Cameron,

This is the first time I have written a letter addressed to both of you. I hope you know how much Grandpa Carl and I love you. Your family is huge, and it is filled with people who love you very much. Never forget that you are my heartbeats – which is why I proudly wear my beautiful rose gold K & C necklace.

Last month, on Kendall's eighth birthday, we were all very excited about the Presidential election. The entire country has been following the news, and people stood in long lines to vote early to cast their ballots. As you both know, because your parents are attorneys and very involved in the Washington, D.C. community, the right to vote is a privilege and a civic responsibility our family takes seriously. I have so many pictures of you with your parents headed to the polls, campaigning with your dad to get out the vote in Philadelphia, and cheering in front of the television for candidates who our family believes will do the best job. Kendall, not every little girl has appeared in social media posts with an actual, real-life vice president – especially the first female VPOTUS running to become POTUS. But you have, and I am mightily impressed with your civic engagement and understanding of what it means to be a democracy.

I know your parents let you stay up a little later last night as the votes were being counted. You were so excited about the prospect of history being made. You've told me how much you love reading about history, especially the stories of women who have achieved remarkable accomplishments. I have no doubt that one day we will be reading about the awesome things you and Cameron have done. When we woke up this morning, the news reports revealed an outcome that was not what we had worked toward, hoped for, and prayed for. I think you may be feeling a bit sad today, especially as you and Cameron pass by the Vice President's home on your way to school. I am writing you this letter to explain why I know our sadness will pass.

We must not give up hope or allow our dreams and wishes for the world to be dashed. Preserving the environment, feeding the hungry, finding medical cures, and protecting our civil rights are all worth fighting for. You two represent Generation Alpha. Your family believes in YOU. Just as you work hard in school and play fair during your softball and soccer games, always do the same wherever you find yourself. In the days to come, you may hear grown-ups talking about the election and who won and who did not. Their voices may sound angry, or their words may seem negative. In our country, based on the democratic principles and rule of law that we believe in, we accept election results, even when we might be disappointed or want the other person to win.

There is, however, something you should be aware of. We humans are not perfect, although we are all God's children. Too often, people draw conclusions and make assumptions about others they do not know., Some people can be selfish, mean, and judgmental. They avoid talking to people they do not know or who may look different than their own family members. That's when something called prejudice surfaces and spoils opportunities to help, share, and learn from one another. You may have heard your parents speak about racism – actions by one group of people targeting another group solely because of the color of their skin. Racism is ugly, it hurts, and it is wrong.

Gigi wants you to remember that no matter what someone else may say or do, even if it's mean and hurts your feelings, that you are smart, special, and worthy. Your life matters! Be grateful and willing to share your blessings – which are vast – with others, especially those less fortunate than you are. Always ask questions and seek answers. Pursue justice, be curious, and kind. Lead with confidence and grace. Dream and imagine, and try new things. Meet new people and visit new places. When you pray for your family, friends, and our country, also include those who don't act in the ways that you do. They need our prayers, too.

Finally, my dear grandchildren, never lose your joy, hope, ambition, and zeal for life. Hold on to your dreams and believe, as I do, that things always work out. One day, either one or both of you might become POTUS or something even more amazing! How do I know this? Because... I believe in YOU!

Love, Gigi

Gail Tusan Washington

Conversation Starters for Generation Alpha and Their Elders

(Posed by Kendall and Cameron's Great-Grandmother, Whisperer Lois Tusan)

1. Have you ever received a letter from one of your elders?

2. How did/would you feel to get one?

3. Why should people vote?

4. What do you do if your candidate does not win?

5. What are your dreams for the world?

6. What can the POTUS do to make things better?

7. What can you do to make the world a better place?

6

A Call to God's Children: Survival and Coping Strategies

by

E. Paulette Smith-Epps

Movement, racial integration, and discrimination in all aspects of their lives.

Family history, oral or written, is an excellent source of survival skills. How did they live and under what circumstances? Family members will be able to talk to you about departed loved ones that you may have never known. There are rich stories of how these relatives paved the way for you. What coping skills did they exhibit that made it possible for you to thrive? Please find out how they navigated those turbulent times and overcame them.

Daily Meditation and Prayer

Read your Bible. Dust it off and start reading. There is so much to learn. I realize that this could be a daunting idea. However, there are Bible guides and concordances that can help you identify Bible passages to guide you through a day. You may approach the Bible in a variety of ways on any given day.

Access daily written devotionals. They can be found in published books, pamphlets, and online meditations written by respected authors. They are usually based on specific scriptures and a narrative on a particular theme. These prepared devotionals often prompt you to reflect on and appreciate your life. They are traditionally a jump start to get an individual thinking about their life and their relationship with God. I recommend reading these with your Bible in hand, referencing the identified scripture, the narrative, and meditating on them. Many of them have recommended scripture readings that will help you complete reading the whole Bible in a year. These devotionals provide something to reflect on throughout your day. The idea is to read the Bible daily.

Appreciate nature

Nature is God's playroom. Please go out and enjoy it. God has created this Earth for our pleasure and enjoyment. Everything in nature is God's way of showing us beauty and peace as we appreciate His handiwork. We cannot create anything in nature. God made all things for our well-being, care, and peace. Human beings are a part of His creation. We are here to benefit from what God has given us. It is up to us to appreciate, protect, and benefit from His creation. As we understand, take a look at the colors, the types of creatures, plants, and animals. If we concentrate and observe, we realize how infinite God is and how finite we are.

Be Self-Aware

Attend to your self-care and personal needs. Self-care is one of the most important things that we can do for ourselves. It is clearly understood that if we do not take care of ourselves, we cannot take care of others, nor can we function healthily.

Speak to a counselor regularly to be sure that your mental and emotional health is well and under control.

Ensure that you are managing your physical health and well-being. See your personal care physician frequently. Stay current on all appointments. Make sure that your dental health is excellent.

Random Acts of Kindness

Think of others. This does not necessarily require an expense. Examples include helping a neighbor pick up trash in their yard, volunteering to take someone to the doctor, grocery shopping for an elderly person, or babysitting to give a parent free time to take care of themselves. Read to an elderly person who may be confined at home. Be creative as you think about others.

Stay Connected to a Faith-Based Group

This could mean attending church regularly each week and participating in auxiliaries and other activities that the church provides. Additionally, it may involve becoming involved with different organizations whose primary purpose is to care for and pray for their members and others. These groups are service-based, which could include food pantries, perused clothing closets, etc. Members of these groups share similar needs, goals, and ideals.

Finally, my younger sisters and brothers, I pray that you will find peace, love, joy, and a stress-free life as you navigate the unsettling and chaotic world around you. Be blessed in the Name of Jesus.

E. Paulette Smith-Epps

WHO ARE WE

A poem written in celebration of Black History Month 2019

— E. Paulette Smith-Epps

Who are we? We are the source of life from the depths of the African continent, where life began.

Who are we? We are the ones who survived the degradation of the holocaust and the genocide of American slavery.

Who are we? We are the strong ones, the builders, the architects, and the planners of this country. We helped build the White House and laid out the city of Washington, DC.

Who are we? We are the intelligent ones. We are engineers and designers, rocket scientists and astronauts, doctors and lawyers, educators and writers, politicians and Supreme Court justices, sports figures and entertainers, movie makers and actors, opera singers and band leaders, fashion and footwear designers, police officers and policewomen, adventurers and inventors.

Who are we? We are families. We are mothers,

fathers, and children. We are husbands and wives, aunts, uncles, and cousins. We are everyone and everybody.

Who are we? We are the warriors. We are the ones who help keep our country safe from war's alarms. We are the non-violent fighters for civil and equal rights under the law.

Who are we? We are people of color who are essential to America. There would not be an America as we know it without our tenacity, endurance, and perseverance.

WHO ARE WE!!!

We are Americans,

We are Americans,

WE ARE AMERICANS!

February 2019

Questions

1. Are you feeling stressed?

2. How do you alleviate stress in your life?

3. What strategies can you use when you are stressed?

4. Do you feel rudderless? Not sure where to find your anchors?

5. What are your concerns during uncertain times?

7

A Call to a Young Friend

by

Henrietta Stith Andrews (Rev.)

> *"You and you alone are the only person*
> *that can live the life that writes the story*
> *that you were meant to tell."*
> **— Kerry Washington**

> *"So, when you're told that your rage is*
> *reactionary,*
> *Remind yourself that rage is our right. It*
> *teaches us it is time to fight."*
> **— Amanda Gorman,**

My Dear Young Friend,

It was a night filled with anxiety as I watched and listened to the increasing number of electoral votes being attributed to Mr. Trump. Long before the results were announced, I turned the TV off and went to bed with a sense of foreboding. The next morning, I took my time reconnecting with the news. I was not eager to have my hunch confirmed that he had won.

Weeks earlier, I could have predicted the outcome had I been willing to proclaim with certainty a hard truth I felt others tiptoed around. The United States of America, despite hard-won progress on racial issues, was not prepared to elect a competent and ethical Black Woman to the highest position of leadership in this country. Instead, the election made visible deep-seated preferences that were embedded in the country's soul.

The results of the election left me with an indelible feeling of having been diminished as a woman and as a person of color. Once again, in this country, I was not good enough. The message in the election was that it did not matter whether one had a high level of education, the depth and breadth of work experience, or the fact of being a decent person. I heard that message. I saw it reflected in the election results, and it did not sit well with my spirit. As the day progressed, so did an inner tension born of the realization that those abandoned values were important to me.

The question, in that moment, became, *How do I survive these times*? Do I wallow in self-pity created by this reality of feeling devalued? The answer to that question was – No! Then I began to realize that I needed to find a way to move forward—to reclaim myself and do so with grace. I questioned the role of history and soon found myself searching history for clues. So, allow me a creative moment as I manipulate time and generations of people ...*history in this country is messy – fraught with tales of injustices punctuated with dreams of democracy tinged with pushbacks made hopeful by progress for a time followed again by injustices – a pattern repeated – over centuries of births and deaths and prayers and struggles of a wearied but determined people…*

I need to see myself as an integral part of this historical work. I was not present hundreds of years ago, but my ancestors were. I inherited the fruit of their labor, the progress and setbacks they experienced during their lifetimes, which have become part of the fabric of my being. What I do today, every action I take, provides the very essentials needed for future generations to build upon. I am part of the arch of God's time: the past, the present, and the future.

So, my young friend, you did not ask for the musings of an old lady. Humor me as I assume the role of an elder who wishes to whisper in your ear a bit of unsought advice. I hesitate to close without a few suggestions for you to consider.

Keep in mind that what you choose to do with your life, either as an individual or as part of a community, shapes this world. You, too, are an integral part of the arch of existence.

Be clear about what matters to you in this life. Define for yourself who you are. Then, based upon those values, move with confidence. Carry the work of the ancestors embedded in your soul through the struggles and blessings of today to the hope of the future.

Most importantly, remember that being a human being requires interaction with other humans, who, often enough, are so different from one another that it requires a lot of thoughtful introspection to maintain peace. The challenge of our faith and of our democratic society is to learn how to love both self and others. If you accept the challenge to learn how to love, expect that living your life will feel like two steps forward when you love well and one step backward when you don't. However laborious your efforts may seem, they are important, and when blended with the efforts of others, they may ultimately bring us to a place of peace imagined by our ancestors and our Creator.

Remember, my friend, to make good decisions and go forth with God's blessing into all your tomorrows.

Henrietta Stith Andrews (Rev.)

Seven Talking Points or Reflective Questions for The Reader

1. The writer mentions racism as one reason people did not vote for Vice President Harris. What other reasons might be attributed?

2. Describe a time in which you felt diminished by another person or situation.

3. How do you respond to the statement, "I believe that what I do today, every action I take, provides the very essentials needed for future generations to build upon?"

4. What does "self-definition" mean to you?

5. What actions are associated with loving (not romantic love) another person?

6. One definition of arch reflects the ongoing relationship between the divine and humanity. In this letter, "arch" additionally imagines a continuous connection from former generations continuing through us to our descendants and beyond. Do you believe that you are part of the

arch of time? How might this way of thinking affect your way of being?

7. What are your gifts that contribute to the shaping of this world?

8

A Call to My Comrades

by

MAJ Zeresh Gosha

> *"Please remember what's at stake. Remember the men and women who have fought and died so that we can live under the rule of law, not the rule of men."*
> — **Liz Cheney**

My Fellow Comrades,

As a member of the Armed Forces, an Army Nurse, and a Veteran, I have been affected by the political climate. Being steeped in a family of volunteer political activism, I had hoped to one day contribute my time and service as a campaign volunteer. This past campaign year, 2024, my goal was brought to fruition. I worked at my county's district headquarters, which is a pivotal democratic county. I was fortunate to meet noted Veteran congressmen, representatives, and a former President. However, I was dismayed to discover that a significant number of my Comrades supported candidates with views and policies that were not in alignment with military values and lacked support for service members.

Impact on Our Democracy

As a Veteran who took my oath to serve and protect my Country seriously, I wondered, Do my Comrades who are voting for someone who will dismantle the military, putting our country in danger, really love our land, the United States of America (USA)? Over time, I have come to realize that differing political views have strained my relationships with fellow members of the Armed Forces. Even friends whom I care deeply about and believe care about me have chosen to support candidates whose beliefs contradict all that we hold dear and what we swore to protect and defend. Navigating these differences has not always been easy and has led to thoughtful reflection on our values and shared experiences.

Not until now could I understand how Hitler came to power and how authoritarianism can impact society by taking over and/or weakening democratic institutions. We are witnessing our freedoms steadily erode, and as the boundaries of the law blur, uncertainty and apprehension can take root throughout our society.

I pray for my friends who may be unconsciously (or consciously) supporting a way of governing that is more in alignment with authoritarianism than democracy.

It can be a challenge for me to stay objective and not let frustration take over, but I know I must remain in prayer – reminding myself that God is in control and He takes care of his children.

Impact on Health and Well-being

Despite my resolve to remain faithful, I can't ignore today's rebellious and unpredictable climate. I've had to tighten my household budget. To help stretch my resources, I rely on the nearby Army installation for groceries and other necessities, just as many other retirees and Veterans do, traveling considerable distances for the opportunity. But I can't help but wonder: if this Military installation were to close, how would that affect our financial stability? What additional actions would I need to take? What other retail establishments would I be required to consider? These thoughts are contributing to the symptoms of my Post-Traumatic Stress Disorder (PTSD). My PTSD has surged due to the recent adverse actions weakening our Fighting Force, the various policy changes, and the increase in lawless conduct within our society. The memories of caring for wounded Soldiers—their shattered lives and the loss I witnessed—have resurfaced in my dreams with renewed intensity. Though I am now retired and no longer subject to recall for Active Duty, my thoughts remain with those who will be sent into combat and those dedicated to providing care for the injured.

I am reminded in these times of President Abraham Lincoln's powerful words from his second inaugural address in 1865: "To care for him who shall have borne the battle, and for his widow, and his orphan..." These words expressed President Lincoln's vision of the moral obligation to support the soldiers who fought and served, along with their families who suffered losses. This sentiment led to the creation of the Department of Veterans Affairs. Today, however, the commitment, support, resources, and unity to those who have served the USA feel uncertain. I, along with millions of Soldiers and their dependents, belong to the Department of Veterans Affairs. We depend on their services for our livelihood and healthcare. As the climate is rapidly changing and Project 2025 is being implemented, I ponder what my comrades were thinking, or even if they were familiar with Project 2025 and its potential impact on the military. I'm blessed to have received my cancer care from the VA Hospital and its civilian healthcare stakeholders. My Breast Cancer Journey was complicated, and continuity of care throughout its duration was critical to my positive outcome. By God's

Grace and an outstanding healthcare team, I am alive. I pray that all my comrades who need healthcare can experience the superb care that I received. However, there is an ongoing threat to the quality of care and subsequent optimal level of functioning provided to patients: supply and staffing budgets in hospitals and clinics have been significantly reduced.

Travel reimbursement has also been reduced. I travel three hours to my VA Healthcare facility to get the best possible care. It is a strain on my budget, but I must incur financial hardship to maintain my optimal level of care. I am Blessed to have private insurance to absorb some of the cost; however, I am concerned for my fellow Comrades who do not have private insurance coverage and are totally dependent on our VA Healthcare System.

Final Thoughts

Despite my unwavering commitment to our country, I must admit that the disparity between the lack of support for our military and the oath taken to serve it leaves me deeply concerned. I realize, though, that I must avoid and resolve the stressors that have been subjugated upon me since the symptoms of PTSD can contribute to the development of Cancer. As such,

I am committed to taking my prescribed medication and keeping all medical appointments, doing yoga and engaging in stress-reducing exercises, and most importantly, praying to God to forgive and deliver us as a Nation, and from ourselves because, as I stated, "God is in control," which gives me solace.

MAJ Zeresh Gosha

Reflective Questions

1. How can differences in political beliefs among veterans and service members affect camaraderie, teamwork, and mutual respect?

2. Do recent shifts in government support impact your personal sense of security and overall well-being?

3. How would continual reductions to resources, facilities, and healthcare services for veterans influence the long-term quality of care and support available?

4. What could be the impact of resource reductions on the effectiveness of our armed forces? Could there be security implications for our country?

9

A Call to Community

by

Beatrice Hunter Pack

> *"Never doubt that a small group of*
> *thoughtful, committed citizens can*
> *change the world: indeed, it's the only*
> *thing that ever has."*
> **— Margaret Mead, Anthropologist.**

Dear Community, Family, and Children,

I feel driven to write to you as I reflect on the unique year of 2024—to express my feelings, anxieties, and, above all, my enduring belief in hope and restoration. I write this letter as a personal reflection and a reminder to all of us that, despite the divisions that have tried us, we are stronger when we stand together.

My year was unlike any other, full of loss, anguish, and uncertainty. Many of us felt like we were navigating a storm without a compass after the events of 2024, which ranged from individual hardships to the communal shock of unexpected national election results. We experienced an unprecedented moment in history: a president stepped down in the middle of his campaign and nominated Vice President Kamala Harris, of Black and Southeast Asian descent. She had only 107 days to prepare for the presidential campaign against Former President Trump. Vice President Harris and former President Trump shared intentions of cutting costs, addressing border control concerns, and building a stronger nation; however, their strategies differed significantly, and news reports revealed discrepancies. Americans were desperately seeking the truth. I found my friends, family, and community distracted, argumentative, and divided, which delayed some of us from achieving our objectives until after the election. I never imagined how separated and strained relationships would become from the turmoil and divisiveness accompanying such a toxic election campaign. Like many voters, I found myself stuck, unsure, and seeking stability as I took breaks from the draining media stories and campaign insults. The news cycles appeared to spiral into discord, fear, and rage, some predicting that the country was descending into anarchy.

Conversations with friends and community members were filled with questions and misgivings. In those moments, I recognized that my wavering may reflect something larger. We were all caught up in a turbulence of misinformation, misconceptions, and dread. Despite it all, I hung onto one thing: hope. It is the foundation of my survival, and I desire it for you.

It is not easy to possess; you must cultivate it – start with a journal of gratitude, reflect on some of your most difficult seasons, and remember the steps you took to healing and rebuilding. If you have healed before, you will find that the possibility of healing and rebuilding is available again. I invite you to try some of the suggestions in this letter and take control of what you can do to help yourself and your community. Get involved in local events and town hall meetings, and continue to educate yourself – you may be surprised to find your involvement can shift your perspective from fear to faith.

The three main topics that dominated my talks and thoughts at the time are what I want to share with you. They are about fear, religion, gender, and culture—subjects that can serve as building blocks for communities or, if misunderstood, can tear them apart. My hope for this letter is to reflect on how we became divided, reconnect with each other, and rebuild with unity and strength in mind.

Fear

During the election, many of us were driven by fear to shut down due to the concept of political smoke and mirrors, which conceals or exaggerates the truth of a situation with misleading or unrelated information. When people are deceived, they move in emotional desperation, and no one is safe when a threat is perceived. Deceit is a common denominator of fear and was used throughout history. I was taught about the ruins of deceit as a youngster during Sunday school. We read from the book of Genesis, chapter three, BC, that God instructed Adam and Eve not to eat of the tree of the knowledge of good and evil. She was deceived by the serpent's lies and driven by the fear of not knowing what was true. Eve's desire to be like God, knowing good and evil, compelled her to eat from the forbidden tree. Eve's decision and her influence on Adam's disobedience led to the consequences of sin, including self-reliance instead of reliance on God, which resulted in subsequent destruction. Our fears peaked throughout the election campaign as topics ranged from price gouging to gender identity, women's rights, and immigration. Americans sought truth amidst the smoke and mirrors - how will the new administration affect our lives? Will the candidates' threats and predictions create more division, mistrust, lies, and chaos? Will it lead to destructive acts, like the attack on the U.S. Capitol building in Washington, D.C., on January 6, 2021? Fear stopped some Americans from exercising their right to vote. Fear continues to manifest in politics, society, and our households. It is time to make America feel safe again. Fear has been used as a tool for division, pitting neighbor against neighbor. Fear is a scream for understanding. It is an invitation to fully listen to each other, understand each other's stories and experiences, and establish a tolerable common ground. As we rebuild, we must remember that bravery is not the absence of fear, but the willingness to face, comprehend, and transform it into courage. Love casts out fear; God has not given us a spirit of fear but of power, love, and a sound mind. I challenge you to get involved in community events at your favorite church and educate yourself on local legislators and politicians by typing https://www.house.gov/representatives in your browser.

Religion versus Moral Character

Religion and morality frequently found themselves at a crossroads in 2024. In a society founded on the principles of liberty, we have seen religion used both as a source of comfort and an instrument of division. Some exploited their religious beliefs to justify exclusion, while others held onto their faith as a source of hope in the face of upheaval. But I realized that religion, in its most fundamental form, is about love, compassion, and moral integrity. What defines us is not the labels we wear or the prayers we say but the compassion we give, the justice we seek, and the integrity we demonstrate. For our nation to rebuild, we must move beyond the restraints of judging one another and seek understanding and common ground that are rooted in truth. We can find areas of connection, acceptance, and tolerance when our minds and hearts are open to do the work. Facing my fears with courage and keeping an open mind led me to lasting relationships with people outside of my religious beliefs. We found parity in some of our difficult conversations; we allowed love to prevail. Now, I encourage you to attend a class to learn more about different religions and the development of moral character. Dare to discover what we have in common with others and work toward building a foundation anchored in truth. It could change your perspective and humanize the unknown in others. If you're looking to explore different regions and develop your moral character, consider checking out your local library's newsletters. You can also find festivals, concerts, exhibits, and church outreach groups for more information.

Gender, Culture, and Identity

Ultimately, I continue to feel and hear the ongoing discussions surrounding gender, culture, and how we present ourselves in the world. These discussions often became battlefields in 2024. Neighborhoods, churches, and communities struggled to determine viable human rights. Rights inherent to us all, regardless of nationality, sex, national or ethnic origin, color, religion, language, or any other status. The Universal Declaration of Human Rights (UDHR) was adopted by the UN General Assembly in 1948 as the first legal document to set out the fundamental human rights to be universally protected. You may find its 30 articles at https://www.ohchr.org/en/what-are-human-rights. Individuals were hesitant to define their beliefs regarding gender, culture, or identity. During my conversations, I discovered hesitancy, intensity, and apprehension were the root of their fear as we searched for ways to fit into an increasingly divided society. The discussion of gender and culture has always been a hot topic of tension, but I have come to understand that these differences are not what divides us—they are what make us whole. It is in our diversity that we built a thriving country and communities. The challenges we face are understanding one another's identities, which are not insurmountable; they are a must for survival. When love prevails, it casts out fear and begins the movement of change, and I believe God is love. I am a Black woman, born on the East Coast.

I attended diverse schools with large populations of Italian families. My mother encouraged us to attend summer camps and join the Girl Scouts to gain a better understanding of leadership and community. I feared being ostracized because of my skin color and cultural differences. However, my mother's support gave me the courage to try new adventures, which helped me learn to socialize with people who were culturally different in my pursuit of parity. At camp, I discovered that our scout troops shared similar beliefs about family, and I learned to appreciate different food choices. These simple things — fellowship, family, and food — brought us closer as a community. We became comfortable enough to introduce other family members, sit at the dinner table together, and share stories that fostered understanding and stronger relationships.

Understanding offers acceptance for growth, knowledge, and empathy. As rebuilders, we must acknowledge the power and strength of each human experience and commit to respecting, caring, and empowering one another. We are on the road to rebuilding our nation and rediscovering the fact that people, not just policy, fuel America. Reflecting on our popular individual votes, the gap was less than two percent. I am hopeful that we, the people, can bridge the gap as we work to find common ground and truth. Let us start the conversation about issues we agree on – healthcare, economics, social security, jobs, and having a safe place for tough collaborations with a focus on solutions.

As you read and reflect, remember the resilience of the American spirit—the very spirit that has carried us through unimaginable grief, uneven playing fields, lost love, and betrayal. Believe that you have the resilience, love, and vision to continue overcoming and rebuilding from division to unity. Our present circumstances are not the end of the story; they are the beginning of recovery for a nation that is exhausted. Again, get involved in your local community groups, churches, and non-profit organizations that support a cause you believe can help restore a healthy and safe America for all. Volunteer for groups that change the laws that make us feel unsafe, unseen, and devalued, and for candidates who champion the causes you believe in!

You have the power to turn the page and create a future that is united, not in our uniformity, but in our shared purpose. I hope that together, we can make a world that is kinder, more just, and more united. I pray that each day, you choose to be hopeful, get involved, and remain committed to driving change. And never give up.

> *"I know we have to have people of good conscience who stand up against oppression. I know we have to have people who understand that social justice belongs to us all. And that wakes me up every morning, and that makes me fight even harder."*
> **— Stacey Abrams**

"There comes a time when one must take a position that is neither safe, nor politic, nor popular, but he must take it because conscience tells him it is right."
The Honorable Martin Luther King

"God Bless America, and may God Bless You!"

Beatrice Hunter Pack

Questions to Reflect On

1. Will you take on the challenge of forming a support group of dedicated and involved citizens to discuss suggestions for restoring and renewing America?

2. Your role can be critical because your experience and insight matter. What will this group look like?

3. How are you managing the conflicts in our news reporting channels? Our collective efforts can make a difference in understanding this complex landscape of media sharing.

4. What did you feel when Bill Owens, executive producer of 60 Minutes, resigned, citing concerns about journalistic independence?

5. Consider the power of your individual actions. If you could change one thing in our political environment, what would it be?

6. If you have not voted, I urge you to consider the power of your vote. It is crucial in shaping our nation's future. Will you take on this responsibility and why?

10

A Closing Reflection

by

Leslie Hazle Bussey

Audre Lorde wrote, "Poetry is not a luxury. It is a vital necessity of our existence. It forms the quality of light within which we predicate our hopes and dreams toward survival and change, first made into language, then into ideas, then into more tangible action."

The foregoing collection of letters is de facto poetry by Audre Lorde's definition. It is, in its totality, a nuanced and deeply human portrait in a historical moment of dehumanization.

The choice of using letters as a vehicle for these messages makes this collection even more directed, more powerful, and more purposeful, as it has given us, as readers, the chance to witness a private and special connection between the authors and the recipients of the letters, while also making us recipients ourselves. So, every worry expressed is a worry for us. Every wish for good is a wish for us. Every word of encouragement is an encouragement to us.

In this final reflection on making sense of this collection and in the privilege of shaping how the reader might be transformed—and in doing so, embody the hope of this powerful gathering of women to change the world—I offer this poem to highlight the intersection of wisdom and whispering.

I invite you to notice the wisdom and whisperers who appear on your path and acknowledge them. I invite you to discover and cultivate the wisdom and the whisperer within yourself. And write a letter or two.

Who is Wisdom?

Wisdom is a letter.

A letter happens when we are holding someone in our hearts and minds

We are thinking of them

And out of our hearts, toward someone,

Flows a yearning

a message

a hope

That we can somehow traverse

The wide valley of

Time, space, air

Storms, blood, love

Skin, death, sunrises

And perform the miracle of

Planting the message of our heart

In the garden within our someone

Hoping that it lands with enough clarity and fidelity
that they feel it like we felt it. Wisdom is a whisperer.

To hear a whisper

We have to lean in and block out noise

Receive the intimacy of breath

Into the ear

Into the heart

Where a confidence, that is,

An instance of confiding

A secret or truth that is not for everyone

Might be held gently and with reverence.

A whisperer is one who whispers

Who chooses not to shout

Not to use force

But to use a velvet weapon nonetheless

Because even when there is danger

Even when one must be quiet to avoid detection

A whisper can be used to convey

Life-giving information

Encouragement

Intelligence

Wisdom is relentless.

Not naive

Not foolish

Not domineering

But resolute

Knowing that our power is in speaking our words, amplifying our stories, and pouring out our love. Knowing that the reason we are still here is not because we were never knocked down, not because we haven't been shattered on the cold bathroom floor, tear-soaked and paralyzed by fear, it's that we have

And we will

Keep.

Getting.

Up.

Wisdom wins.

A GUIDE FOR CONVERSATION

Conversation provides an opportunity for people to address critical issues in all settings where humans gather. Conversations are easier when points of view are shared. More often effective conversations among people with varying views requires intentional work for all involved.

WHAT IS A CONVERSATION?

The sharing of ideas between two or more people where one is the speaker and the other the listener. and where there may be no agreement about the subject matter.

For conversation to be successful:

The Speaker

1. Allows a moment of pause before talking rather than jumping in too quickly.

2. Makes "I" statements rather than "You" statements.

3. Make no judgements about people or what has been said.

4. Makes eye contact and maintain an appropriate facial expression.

5. Pays attention to the length of time one is talking.

The Listener

1. Has unconditional positive regard for the speaker.

2. Listens with empathy as if you genuinely care.

3. Maintains an open body language. How you sit or stand, the position of your arms or what you do with your hands may send unintended messages.

Both speaker and listener must be:

- Mindful of the situation in the room and able to adjust your conversation accordingly.

- Willing to seek common ground and build on shared interests.

- Respectful of boundaries.

- Interested enough to seek the other person's opinion.

- Ask open-ended questions.

A good conversation requires skill that either comes naturally or must be practiced. Most of us will need to practice. To that end, choose one rule to concentrate on until it becomes second nature then move to another rule. Be patient with yourself as your new behaviors become natural responses.

THE WISDOM WHISPERERS BIOS

Henrietta Stith Andrews

Henrietta Stith Andrews is a retired ordained minister with the United Church of Christ living in Powder Springs, Georgia. She is a graduate of Yankton College and earned a Master's in Early Childhood Education from Case Western Reserve University and a Master's of Divinity from Lancaster Theological Seminary. In 2010, she completed the Dominican Center for Religious Development Graduate Program in Spiritual Direction. Henrietta is the mother to Catherine (deceased) and Stephen Jr. She is the grandmother to Elijah. A self-taught artist and poet, and the author of *My Short Hair Tells It All* (2016), she delights in creating handmade quilts, abstract wall hangings, paper houses made of reused materials, and clothespin dolls.

Leslie Hazle Bussey

Leslie Hazle Bussey is the CEO and Executive Director of the Georgia Leadership Institute for School Improvement (GLISI). This nonprofit organization designs transformational leadership experiences for successful schools and thriving communities. Leslie has raised over $23 million in foundation and grant funds, led groundbreaking work in developing leaders' social-emotional competencies, and increased board diversity by 50%. Since 2023, she has been the lead architect of RETAIN (Restoring Teacher Aspiration and Innovation), a two-year initiative aimed at developing leaders' social-emotional competencies as a pathway to positively impact teacher working conditions.

Drawing on her experience as a teacher of middle-grade students in Lusaka, Zambia, Leslie previously served as Director of Research for Learning-Centered Leadership at the Southern Regional Education Board and Project Director at the Mass Networks Education Partnership. She currently serves on the Kennesaw

State University Bagwell College of Education Board of Visitors, the advisory board of SEL4GA, and is a member of the Expert Team for Georgia's Statewide Literacy Coaching Model. Additionally, she is a mentor in the GEM (Georgia Education Mentorship) Program. She is a graduate of the Harvard Business School Strategic Perspectives in Non-Profit Management program as well as Leadership Atlanta (Class of 2023).

In her free time, Leslie loves yoga and cooking. She also runs but has not yet learned to love it. It is useful, though, to keep up with her 10-year-old son, Oliver, and her older children, Jordan (24) and Ava (19).

Joan Drescher

Joan Drescher is a wife, mother, mother-in-law, and grandmother. She holds a B.S. degree in Sociology from Appalachian State University in Boone, NC. Her best and most rewarding job was raising her two children. She is the author of the children's book Penguins, Pizza, and Other Poems. She is currently working on another book, You Know You are a Grandmother

When…Being a grandma is definitely right up there with raising her children. She enjoys her time at Children's Healthcare of Atlanta as a volunteer with CURE Childhood Cancer. She and her husband live in Decatur, Georgia, and enjoy traveling, cooking, and spending time with their family. With two current grandkids and two on the way, they are looking forward to exciting and more spoiling opportunities ahead.

Joyce Coleman Edwards

Joyce Edwards is a Project Manager with EY Technology (Ernst & Young LLP). In this role, she manages several initiatives with new and updated Microsoft applications. She is also a facilitator for the Learning team's Welcome to EY sessions, providing services for new employees. She brings a wealth of professional experience, having worked in the public, private, and governmental sectors, as well as in non-profit and major corporations. As a business administrator, her skill set includes administration, marketing, entrepreneurial technical assistance, and project management. She is an active member of Leadership Atlanta and First Congregational Church, where she serves as a Deacon. She enjoys reading and is a member of the Turning Leaf Book Club. She and her husband, Johnny L. Edwards, a local architect, have been married for 30 years and have traveled the world together. They have three sons and five grandchildren.

Zeresh Gosha

Zeresh Gosha is a retired Registered Nurse with 37 years of experience, including nurse educator, military, and civilian nursing. She earned a BA in Biology from Talladega College, a Bachelor of Science in Nursing and an Associate Degree in General Studies from Columbus College, and a Master of Science in Nursing from Troy State University. She began her nursing career as an Adult Health Nurse in the civilian sector, with a particular affinity for teaching hospitals. With the nursing skills she acquired, Zeresh confidently became a travel nurse, working in several states across the country, including Delaware and Texas. As an Assistant Professor of Nursing, she taught at notable colleges, including Tuskegee University. Upon graduating from nursing school, Zeresh joined the Army Nurse Corps to humbly and earnestly serve her country. She was able to render care to her wounded Comrades, starting as a Staff Nurse and then being promoted to Head Nurse at Walter Reed National Military Medical Center during the Operation Iraqi Freedom / Operation Enduring Freedom War during the heat of the battle. Zeresh has been fortunate to engage in grant writing and implementation during her role as a nurse educator. One of her greatest accomplishments was being blessed to fulfill her desire to implement missionary work when she embarked on a medical mission to Cap-Haïtien, Haiti. Now, as a retiree, she volunteers at a non-profit primary care clinic. Her me time encompasses spending time with family and friends, traveling, exercising, and engaging in various arts activities.

Donna Akiba Sullivan Harper

An internationally recognized Langston Hughes scholar, Akiba Harper taught English at Spelman College from 1987 to 2020 and is now Professor Emerita. Nationally, she served as President of the College Language Association from 2018 to 2020. She was a founding member and past president of the Langston Hughes Society. She currently serves on the Advisory Board for UNCF-Mellon.

A Phi Beta Kappa graduate of Oberlin College, Akiba Harper earned her M.A. and Ph.D. from Emory University.

An ordained Presbyterian elder, she is an active member of Monday night Bible study at First Congregational Church of Atlanta.

Rosalyn Roberts Mack

Rosalyn Roberts Mack is a retired corporate executive with 34 years of experience in sales, marketing, project management, and business leadership. She earned a BS in Chemical Engineering from Howard University and an MBA from Rutgers University. She is also a proud Life Member of Alpha Kappa Alpha Sorority, Inc. While working in corporate America, she participated in many company-sponsored activities designed to identify, learn, and respect cultural differences. Her involvement spanned over a decade, resulting in the development and management of inclusive, equitable, and high-performing business teams. An ordained deacon at First Congregational Church UCC in Atlanta, GA, she served in this role for over 12 years. In her spare time, she enjoys attending continuing education courses, writing, exercising, attending live music shows, and traveling globally with her beloved husband, Trentton, whom she has been with for over 34 years. They have two amazing adult children, Victoria and Joshua. She and her husband live on

Amelia Island, FL, and enjoy hosting family and friends there, as well as in Roswell, GA.

Beatrice Hunter Pack

Beatrice Hunter Pack is a wife, mother, and grandmother who embraces her calling. She enjoys life coaching and helping people overcome their fears and uncertainties. She is drawn to individuals, especially those who are misunderstood, and believes that everyone has a story about coming to terms with themselves. Her motto is *kindness before judgement.* Over the course of her 43-year career, she led and managed executive sales teams, developed marketing innovations, and established business initiatives. Beatrice is dependable and known for her hospitality, healthy eating, and the thrill of the hunt in shopping. However, community service, prayer, and family remain at her core. She resides in the Midwest with her husband and enjoys their travel adventures.

Michèle Mateno Silatchom

Michèle Mateno Silatchom is a first-generation French Citizen with roots in Cameroon (Central Africa) who has been living in the US for eight years. With a legal background, Michèle has over 20 years of professional experience in not-for-profit organizations, law firms, consulting companies, and as a self-employed individual. She has always been curious about questions related to globalization, especially its sociological effects on people. In this volume, Michèle writes about the elections that have shaped her life and the epiphany she experienced following the results of the 2024 elections. In her spare time, she enjoyed cooking, eating, travelling, and discovering the various wonders of this world.

E. Paulette Smith-Epps

E. Paulette Smith-Epps, a native Atlantan, is the daughter of a Baptist minister and an educator. She grew up in Atlanta with three brothers. She was educated in the Atlanta Public School System, Spelman College, and Atlanta University. Paulette is a professional librarian who was Assistant Director of Public Services when she retired from the Atlanta-Fulton Public Library System. Currently, she works as a Media paraprofessional in an elementary school. She is a member of St. Paul's Episcopal Church in Atlanta, Georgia, where she is a lay reader. She enjoys singing, listening to music, reading, writing, and traveling the world. Paulette is the mother of three children. She has four grandchildren and four godchildren. Paulette is the widow of William Given Epps, Sr., and lives and works in Atlanta, Georgia.

Gail Tusan Washington

Gail Tusan Washington is a Senior Superior Courts Judge, as well as an arbitrator and mediator with the national dispute resolution company, JAMS. First writing under the pen name, Susan Washington, she published her debut novel, Misjudged, and the sequel, Riley, The Judge's Son. Gail's joy in facilitating creative collaboratives led to the formation of the Wisdom Whisperers collective and the Loving Wisdom anthologies were born. She also serves as the founder and board president of The Pave Foundation, Inc. This nonprofit entity encourages Black girls to "dream in STEAM" through its signature summer camp, annual Super Science Day of the Girl, and other enrichment activities. Gail and her husband, Carl, live in Atlanta with Sammie, their loyal canine rescue. While Gail generously gives her time to her church and the community at large, she enjoys traveling and playing golf with Carl. Her most precious moments are spent with family. Learn more about Gail at her website, www.gailtusanwashington.com.